GOAL!
LATIN STARS OF
SOCCER

Soccer Star
Kaká

Jeff Burlingame

Speeding Star
Keep Boys Reading!

LIBRARY
WORK

Library of Congress Cataloging-in-Publication Data

Burlingame, Jeff, author.
  Soccer star Kaká / Jeff Burlingame.
    pages cm.
  Includes bibliographical references and index.
  Summary: "This Brazilian footballer has been a rising star since his debut with São Paulo in
2001. In this sports biography, explore Kaká's journey from almost becoming paralyzed to winning
the Ballon d'Or to playing for the historic club Real Madrid"— Provided by publisher.
  ISBN 978-1-62285-230-7
  1. Kaká, 1982– —Juvenile literature. 2. Soccer players—Brazil—Biography—Juvenile
literature. I. Title.
  GV942.7.K35B87 2014
  796.334092—dc23
  [B]

                    2013022533

Future Editions:
Paperback ISBN: 978-1-62285-231-4
EPUB ISBN: 978-1-62285-232-1
Single-User PDF ISBN: 978-1-62285-233-8
Multi-User PDF ISBN: 978-1-62285-234-5

Printed in the United States of America
112013 Bang Printing, Brainerd, Minn.
10 9 8 7 6 5 4 3 2 1

To Our Readers: We have done our best to make sure all Internet addresses in this book were active
and appropriate when we went to press. However, the author and the Publisher have no control over,
and assume no liability for, the material available on those Internet sites or on other Web sites they may
link to. Any comments or suggestions can be sent by e-mail to comments@speedingstar.com or to the
address below.

Speeding Star
Box 398, 40 Industrial Road
Berkeley Heights, NJ 07922
USA
www.speedingstar.com

✪ Enslow Publishers, Inc., is committed to printing our books on recycled paper. The paper in every
book contains 10% to 30% post-consumer waste (PCW). The cover board on the outside of each book
contains 100% PCW. Our goal is to do our part to help young people and the environment too!

Photo Credits: ©AP Images/Alberto Di Lolli, p. 31; ©AP Images/Alberto Pellaschiar, p. 4; ©AP
Images/Alik Keplicz, p. 25; ©AP Images/Andres Kudacki, p. 40; ©AP Images/Antonio Calanni, pp.
11, 14, 17; ©AP Images/Carlo Baroncini, p. 19; ©AP Images/Daniel Ochoa de Olza, pp. 35, 36; ©AP
Images/Eraldo Peres, p. 32; ©AP Images/Koji Sasahara, p. 23; ©AP Images/Luca Bruno, pp. 8, 28,
43; ©AP Images/Marco Vasini, p. 7; ©AP Images/Roberto Candia, p. 20; ©AP Images/Walter Bieri/
Keystone Photostream, p. 27; ©AP Images/Wander Roberto/Agencia Estado, p. 13.

Cover Photo: ©AP Images/Gabriele Putzu/Keystone

CONTENTS

Even though he was widely considered the favorite to win the Ballon d'Or, Kaká was still thrilled to finally hear his name called.

The World's Best

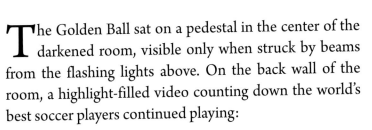

The Golden Ball sat on a pedestal in the center of the darkened room, visible only when struck by beams from the flashing lights above. On the back wall of the room, a highlight-filled video counting down the world's best soccer players continued playing:

"Andrea Pirlo …"
"Didier Drogba …"
"Lionel Messi …"
"Cristiano Ronaldo …"

The minute-long video ended with the number "1" filling up the screen. The lights again flashed on the golden ball as music began. Thirty tension-filled seconds later, the French-speaking announcer finally said the name of 2007's best player:

"Kaká!"

The room lit up, revealing a small crowd seated in a semicircle around the ball. The camera and lights shifted focus to the baby-faced winner. Kaká grabbed the golden soccer ball—formally known as the Ballon d'Or—and offered his acceptance speech. "I want to thank God, who allowed me to be here today," he said. "I thank my wife, my parents, and Milan, the team that allowed me to win. I also thank my teammates, both at Milan and Brazil, and all of the fans. This is very special for me—it culminates an astonishing year."

The twenty-five-year-old midfielder had many wins in 2007 with his teammates. In April, Kaká's outstanding play led his Italian football club, AC Milan, to the title of the Champions League, making them the best team in all of Europe. In fact, Kaká was so dominant in that tournament that most soccer insiders predicted he would easily win the Ballon d'Or later in the year. *France Football* magazine—the publication that awards the Ballon d'Or—reportedly had even told Kaká to be sure to dress nicely and comb his hair for the ceremony, because the award was going to be given to him.

Kaká was nicely groomed when he accepted the award the morning of December 2, 2007, in front of his wife, his brother, and his mother. As his speech continued, he vowed to remain loyal to his adopted city of Milan and its soccer team. "[The Ballon d'Or is] the top prize around and the only way to win something like this is to play for a team like Milan," he said. "It's great to be part of a team that wins."

After the ceremony in Paris, Kaká flew directly back to Milan to celebrate with fans of that winning team. Some two thousand of them had gathered in the city's main square to hear their hero speak. Still wearing his black suit and black tie from earlier in the day, Kaká briefly addressed the crowd. "This is my fifth season here. I have had many

Kaká was able to spend the best years of his career with AC Milan, where he brought them many championships and trophies.

opportunities to walk away, but it is only normal that a Milan player is highly sought after," he said. "I want to become the captain of this [team] and a symbol. My future will be here and I am happy at Milan."

The crowd roared as Kaká took off his jacket. He put his No. 22 red-and-black AC Milan jersey over his shirt and tie, and hoisted the golden ball above his head. As he did so, the crowd sang in unison. It was the same song they sang each time Kaká took to the soccer field:

> *Siam venuti fin qua* [We came here]
> *Siam venuti fin qua* [We came here]
> *Per vedere segnare Kaká* [To see Kaká score]

"Why would I want to change?" Kaká asked.

The joy and happiness that Kaká brought to Milan left a mark on Italy that will never be forgotten.

Becoming Káká

When Ricardo Izecson dos Santos Leite was born April 22, 1982, his hometown of Brasília was not much older than he was. The Brazilian town had been founded just twenty-two years earlier. The capital city was built from scratch in the middle of the desert in an effort to relocate the capital to the center of the country. For nearly two-hundred years prior, Brazil's capital was the city of Rio de Janeiro, located on the country's southeastern coast.

Both of Ricardo's parents worked amongst the more than one million people that called Brasília home. His father, Bosca Izecson Pereira Leite, was a civil engineer. His mother, Simone Cristina dos Santos Leite, was a schoolteacher. Both jobs were good ones, which allowed

Ricardo to avoid dealing with the poverty many of his peers were forced to suffer through. In Brazil, there is a wide gap between the rich and the poor. Ricardo's family was considered upper middle-class.

Ricardo did have to deal with some adversity during his childhood. Much of it was due to the fact that he moved so much. When he was four years old, he and his family moved west across the country to Cuiabá, where his father was sent to work. His new city had less than half as many people as Brasília.

It was not just Ricardo and his parents who made the move. By the time they left Brasília, the family had added another member. Ricardo's younger brother, Rodrigo Izecson dos Santos Leite, had been born October 14, 1985. When he was learning to talk, Rodrigo had a lifelong impact on the way his brother would be known. The younger sibling could not pronounce his older brother's name, or his nickname "Ricardinho" [Little Ricardo]. So he began calling him "Caca." The spelling of the nickname eventually changed to "Kaká," but the name stuck with Ricardo the rest of his life. Little Rodrigo also earned a childhood nickname: Digão.

Kaká lived in Cuiabá for three years, until his father's job brought them back across the country to the southeastern city of São Paulo. Some fifteen million people lived in São Paulo when Kaká and his family arrived there in the late 1980s. It was Brazil's largest city and one of the largest cities in the world. Kaká enrolled in a Baptist elementary school, where he was known as a shy kid who wanted to become a professional tennis player. Tennis remained his sport of choice for most of his first year at the school, but he also played on the school's futsal team. Futsal is a quicker-paced game of soccer played on a smaller field with a smaller ball and with only five players on each team. One day, Kaká's gym teacher saw him play futsal in class and was impressed with the seven-year-old's ability to handle the ball. The teacher told Kaká's parents they should sign him up for the local soccer club to hone his talent. The club's name was Alphaville, and players had to qualify to join.

Being singled out as a soccer player in Brazil is a special achievement. Soccer is by far the country's most favored sport, as it is in the rest of Latin America. Many youngsters grow up dreaming of playing soccer—known as futebol

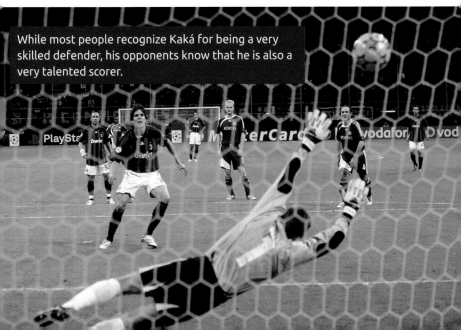

While most people recognize Kaká for being a very skilled defender, his opponents know that he is also a very talented scorer.

[football] in Brazil—professionally. On playgrounds, streets, and beaches across the country, they spend hours impersonating their favorite soccer stars. Those stars included Pelé, a Brazilian who played soccer during the 1950s, 1960s, and 1970s. Many believe Pelé is the best soccer player of all time. In the poorer areas of Brazil, children who cannot afford the proper soccer boots [shoes] or even a ball often can be found barefoot, kicking balled-up rags held together by tape or rope.

Although he initially preferred tennis, Kaká always held soccer in high regard. In fact, he received his first soccer ball as a gift from his parents before he could talk.

Kaká excelled playing soccer for Alphaville. Soon, he was traveling out of Brazil to play with his team in tournaments. In one tournament in nearby Chile, held when he was eleven, Kaká was the leading scorer.

Kaká also was a very religious child, as were his parents. At age twelve, Kaká decided to commit his life to Christianity and get baptized. "When I was baptized in 1994, something supernatural happened to me," Kaká told *Joy!* magazine in 2010. "I cannot explain it, but after that experience I grew closer to God and began to know Him in a more in-depth way. My life changed and was never the same again."

His life on the soccer field, or pitch, was never the same again after he began to train with his hometown São Paulo Football Club. Kaká's dedication to soccer became much stronger. Founded in 1935, São Paulo was one of

Kaká knew growing up that in order to have a successful and promising soccer career, he would have to work extremely hard.

the most successful football teams in Latin America. As with many of the storied European and Latin-American football clubs, São Paulo had a youth program from which it would eventually promote many of its future players. Those young players lived in dormitories during the week and attended classes. In many ways, their lives were just that of typical American college students. The biggest difference—besides age—was that the São Paulo youth also played soccer every day.

Kaká's best friend at the academy was a boy from the large city of Campo Grande. His name was Marcelo Saragosa. Marcelo and Kaká—separated in age by only three months—immediately hit it off. The boys often hung out and studied together during the week. Their

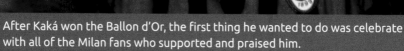
After Kaká won the Ballon d'Or, the first thing he wanted to do was celebrate with all of the Milan fans who supported and praised him.

friendship grew even closer on the weekends. That is when most kids from the academy traveled home to visit their parents. But because Campo Grande was too far for Marcelo to travel, he ended up spending many weekends with Kaká's family in São Paulo.

Kaká was much smaller than other players his age, which led to a slower advancement through São Paulo's youth ranks than he would have liked. He had the ballhandling skills of those years older than he was, but his size often held him back. Many matches, he could be found on the bench while others played. "It was hard, but I learnt to fight for what I wanted," Kaká told *Joy!* magazine.

Kaká's coaches still saw him as a player with great potential. He signed a professional contract with São Paulo when he turned fifteen years old. The team immediately put him on training and diet plans designed to help him get bigger and stronger. Kaká slowly did that, and began to stand out on the field. He led his teams to several big wins, including many championships. Other clubs even began to try to lure him away from São Paulo to come play for them. His training was paying off. He was on track to fulfill the dream of every Brazilian child. It appeared as though Kaká was going to become a professional soccer player. That is, until a devastating accident almost ended not only his soccer career, but his life as well.

chapter 2

Stardom

In October 2000, Kaká was playing for São Paulo's junior team in a championship tournament when he received two yellow-card penalties during a match. The first yellow card was a warning for his conduct. The second yellow card meant he was kicked out of the game and was not allowed to play in the next game, either. Kaká decided to make the most of his disqualification. He went to spend the weekend with his grandparents in the small Brazilian town of Caldas Novas.

The rest of Kaká's family was at his grandparents' house, too. One day, the family decided to visit a local water park. That is where both Kaká's soccer career and his

A quick look and some might think this is Kaká. However, this is actually Kaká's brother, Digão, who is the reason the world knows his brother as "Kaká."

life nearly ended. As Kaká was going down a water slide, he told *The Sun* newspaper in 2007, he "… fell awkwardly and hit my head on the bottom of the pool. I twisted my neck but did not realize at the time that I had broken my sixth cervical bone."

Kaká left the swimming pool with a sharp headache. He also was bleeding from the head. He was taken to the hospital, where his wound was stitched up and he was given an X-ray. No problems were found. So Kaká returned to São Paulo on Monday to continue training with his teammates. On Tuesday, the pain became unbearable and Kaká alerted a trainer. Another X-ray was taken, and this one revealed a broken neck. "Everyone, including the doctors, told me I was very lucky that nothing more serious happened," he told the Web site *Beyond the Ultimate* in 2012. "They told me that I could have become paralyzed and lost my ability to walk and to play soccer. I believe it was not luck. I believe God was protecting me during that time from anything more serious."

Kaká was fitted with a cervical collar and was not allowed to play soccer as he recovered. During those months he spent recovering, Kaká set ten goals for himself. His number one goal was to be able to play soccer again.

The eighteen-year-old achieved that goal in January 2001, when he returned to the pitch to play for the São Paulo junior team. Less than a month later, he achieved another of his ten goals when he was called up to play for São Paulo's main team. In 2012, he told *Beyond the*

Kaká is very open about his religious views, and since he came back from his life-threatening injury, he is sure to thank God every time he steps onto the pitch.

Ultimate: "Because of this, I believe God had a purpose in that accident. It is something that happened just before I had the great blessing of starring as a professional in São Paulo and initiating my career as a professional soccer player."

Kaká immediately made his presence felt on the senior team. In particular, his ability to thread the needle on passes to teammates and his talent for placing the ball into the net in a spot where rival goalkeepers could not get to it. Kaká scored his first goal of the season February 4 against Santos FC in front of fourteen thousand fans in São Paulo's historic home stadium, Morumbi. That goal, which gave São Paulo a 2–1 lead in a game they eventually won 4–2, foreshadowed the greatness he would eventually achieve.

He finished the season with twelve goals in twenty-seven games. Soccer matches often are low-scoring affairs. Oftentimes, one goal will be all that is scored during the entire ninety minutes.

Kaká's best showing came March 7 in front of seventy-two thousand people at Morumbi. It was during the finals of the Rio-São Paulo Tournament. With his team trailing 1–0 to Botafogo with less than eleven minutes left in the game, Kaká scored the game-tying goal. Two minutes later, he scored the game-winning goal. When the ball hit the back of the net, Kaká's teammates ran from their positions across the field and piled on top of him. It was the first time São Paulo had ever won the Rio-São Paulo Tournament. It

While being a fan-favorite is something Kaká holds with high honor, he knew dating would be hard because some people would be more interested in his money and stardom than loyalty and love.

was a big deal not only in São Paulo and Rio but also in the rest of Brazil and beyond. Kaká instantly became a star.

With Kaká's overnight stardom came many challenges. Magazines, newspapers, and television shows began to feature him. Everywhere he went in São Paulo, people would gather around him in search of a handshake or an autograph. Young girls also were fascinated by the dark-haired athlete—who had grown to be more than six feet tall. They cut out magazine pictures and tacked them to their walls. They posted his pictures, masked with hearts and stars, on their social-media Web sites. They wrote him letters. Some asked if they could be his girlfriend. "I get about 50 letters a day and keep them all," Kaká told *ISTOÉ Gente* magazine in 2002. Because of his popularity, he added, "[Sometimes] I dread going outside." Kaká's mother initially replied to every letter her son received but had to quit doing that when the numbers became too great.

Although it may sound like an ideal situation for an unmarried teenager to be in, it was not for Kaká. He wanted to focus on soccer. He believed dating would distract from that focus. If he were to date, Kaká said "loyalty" would be his number one requirement. And his girlfriend would not be someone who knew him because of his soccer achievements.

Kaká's development as a soccer player soon tested his own loyalty to São Paulo when other, better-known European teams began bidding for his services. Those teams hoped the lure of money and more fame could tempt him away from São Paulo. But Kaká was not ready to leave his hometown team—yet.

Instead, he stuck around for the 2002 season, continuing his growth as both a person and a player. His season with São Paulo nearly mirrored his rookie campaign. He was even named the Brazilian League's most valuable player with the Bola de Ouro award. That was an excellent accomplishment, but Kaká's biggest achievement of 2002 was being chosen to play on Brazil's national team. The selection would have been an honor in any year, but in 2002 it was extra special. That is because 2002 was a World Cup year and Brazil—as usual—had qualified to be part of the tournament.

Kaká was the final player selected for the World Cup team. Some reported he was only selected because another player had gotten into trouble with Brazil's coach. But that coach, Luiz Felipe Scolari, said Kaká earned the spot because he was such a good player. The Web site *Realmadrid.com* reported that Scolari had said at the time, "Someone with his talent and characteristics appears once every fifty years. He will soon be a role model for every Brazilian who is called up by the national team."

Held every four years, World Cup is one of the world's biggest sporting events. It is far bigger than baseball's World Series, football's Super Bowl, or tennis' Wimbledon. As its name suggests, the month-long World Cup features teams

Playing for Brazil's national team allowed Kaká to develop friendships with teammates and fellow Ballon d'Or winners Ronaldinho and Ronaldo.

from across the globe. Millions of fans attend its matches and tens of millions more watch on television.

The World Cup was held in stadiums throughout South Korea and Japan. With international superstars such as Ronaldinho and Ronaldo on its roster, Brazil had little use for Kaká when the actual games began. In fact, he only played in one of Brazil's World Cup matches. But he did gain valuable experience in doing so. He also earned a World Cup championship—a feat most soccer players only dream of but never achieve. That championship came June 30, when Brazil beat Germany, 2–0, in front of 69,000 people in Japan. It was Brazil's fifth World Cup win.

Kaká told *Athletes in Action* that being able to play for his national team was a wonderful experience. "It is a sensation that goes beyond words because it is very strong," he said. "The first time I heard the national anthem while standing there with the national team and the entire stadium brought great emotion. It was a huge blessing from God."

Kaká received what he considered to be another blessing that year, too. Through family friends, he was introduced to a young and beautiful Brazilian woman named Caroline Celico. Though she was only fifteen years old, Caroline was somewhat used to celebrities because her mother was a top designer for popular fashion company, Christian Dior. Kaká, who was five years older than Caroline, fell for her and quickly integrated her into his life. Caroline told the blog *Kaká e Carol World*: "When he saw me for the first

Kaká is one of the main reasons that the Brazilian national team has had great success since 2002.

time, I asked him to sign an autograph to my friend and one to me. He wrote to my friend: 'With love, from Kaká,' and to me he wrote: 'Kisses, with love from Kaká.' He told me that he had liked me ever since."

Caroline spent a lot of time with Kaká's family and friends and also attended his church. He even created a nickname for her, "Boo." For a while, the couple was inseparable. Still, soccer always was Kaká's first priority. Shortly after he and Caroline began dating, that priority tore them thousands of miles—and one large ocean—apart.

Top of the World

The same European soccer clubs that had wanted to steal Kaká away from São Paulo after his first professional season in 2001 wanted him even more after his 2002 season. Many teams got into a bidding war for the twenty-one-year-old. They all believed he was a star on the rise that would only get better as he played and matured.

AC Milan, a powerhouse team from the second-largest city in Italy, eventually won out. In 2003, Milan paid São Paulo more than ten million dollars to obtain the rights to Kaká. Milan was not the highest bidder, but it was the team that had always been his favorite European squad. Milan's owner, Silvio Berlusconi, thought highly enough

When Milan won the bidding war for Kaká, they considered the cost they paid to be a steal for the talent they were receiving.

of Kaká's abilities that he told the press that the ten million dollars was mere "peanuts."

In Milan, Kaká found himself under the microscope even more than he had been in Brazil. That was because the best soccer players in the world play in Europe. Fans around the world follow its teams. Kaká was up for the challenge. The expectation was that Kaká would sit on the bench for a while and learn from Milan's star players while he adjusted to Europe's more physical style of play. But Kaká quickly worked his way into the team's starting lineup. He scored his first European goal in Milan's fifth match of the year and found the net ten times in thirty games on the season. That scoring helped lead Milan to its first Italian league title, Serie A, in several years.

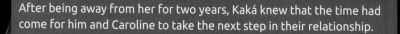

After being away from her for two years, Kaká knew that the time had come for him and Caroline to take the next step in their relationship.

Kaká's production dropped off a bit during the following season, 2004–05. He scored seven goals in thirty-eight games. Milan finished in second place in its league. The year was still a personal success for Kaká. In fact, he was named Serie A Footballer of the Year, the league's player of the year, and also continued to compete for Brazil's national team during the off-season.

While Kaká was in Milan, his girlfriend Caroline remained in Brazil with her parents. She and Kaká had discussed marriage several times but had chosen to wait until she was older. After Kaká had been away for two seasons playing in Italy, they decided they had waited long enough. They did not want to be apart any longer. Two days before his birthday in April 2005, Kaká brought Caroline to Venice, Italy. He told her it was to watch him sign an important document. But when Caroline arrived in the city—considered one of the most romantic in the world—Kaká took her to a hotel and proposed to her on a deck overlooking the city. She said yes.

The couple did not waste time on a long engagement and immediately began planning their wedding. They decided to hold it two days before Christmas 2005 in São Paulo, at the Reborn in Christ Church. It was the same church Kaká had introduced Caroline to years earlier. The wedding was attended by six hundred people, including friends, family, and many of Kaká's current and former teammates, including Adriano, Roberto Carlos, and Ronaldo. During the ceremony, the church's choir sang a song Kaká had written especially for his bride. Kaká's longtime friend, Marcelo Saragosa, was his best man.

Kaká and Caroline honeymooned on the island of Bora Bora in the Pacific Ocean. Caroline then permanently moved to Milan to be with Kaká while he continued his soccer career. Marriage—and the dedication to one partner—was a natural fit for Kaká. He was a very religious person and a member of a devoted group called Athletes of Christ. During games, he often wore T-shirts underneath his uniform that said "I Belong to Jesus." The words "Jesus in First Place" were etched on the side of his cleats. When he scores a goal, he raises his arms straight up in the air to praise Jesus. Kaká had never taken part in the partying, rock-star lifestyles many of his fellow teammates did. "It is not my place to make judgments about the behavior of any other footballer," he told *The Telegraph* in 2007, "[but] cars and women, things like that, have never been important to me. My family, and my belief in God and Jesus are the things which determine my life. I do want to live my life in the right way, and live my life close to God."

Marriage did not seem to slow Kaká's career. His wedding came in the middle of a season in which he scored fourteen goals and appeared in thirty-five league games. In the summer of 2006, he returned to play for the Brazilian national team to help defend the World Cup title the team had won four years earlier. Kaká played a much larger role at the World Cup this time. In 2002, he had only played in one early game. This time, he was a starter in all matches

Growing up, the skills that Kaká learned while playing futsal in gym class were what made him a step faster than his opponents.

Kaká had such a positive impact on his home country that the former president of Brazil, Luiz Inácio Lula da Silva, felt obligated to meet with the superstar.

for the powerful Brazilians, alongside such superstars as Ronaldo and Ronaldinho. Kaká scored Brazil's first goal of the tournament in a 1–0 win over Croatia in the opening match. Brazil easily advanced to the quarterfinals of the 2006 World Cup but ended up losing there, 1–0 to France.

As they had previously done when Kaká was playing for São Paulo, other teams began attempting to lure Kaká from Milan to come play for them. The biggest push came from Spanish team Real Madrid. But Milan knew what they had in the young player and would not give him up. That turned out to be a smart move on Milan's part.

During the 2006–07 season, Kaká led Milan to victory against the best teams in Europe in the Champions League tournament. He was the tournament's top scorer with ten goals in fourteen games. For his effort, Kaká was named most valuable player.

That most valuable player award was just one of many big honors Kaká received in 2007. Several organizations named him their player of the year. Those organizations included soccer's international governing body, FIFA, and *World Soccer* magazine. Kaká's award-winning run also included his December 2007 win of the Ballon d'Or. In the run up to the Ballon d'Or voting, the leading Italian news agency wrote a story quoting several soccer experts who believed Kaká would easily win the award. Kaká's skills were the reason they all listed him. "[He has] superb control and dribbling skills," the story read, "[and] seems to be able to anticipate the intentions of teammates and opponents alike to choose the right pass every time. ... He is also blessed with an explosive turn of pace ... and is a tireless worker whose movement off the ball is as good as it is on it."

Despite all his honors, Kaká remained humble. At the FIFA award ceremony, he said: "When I was a boy, I used to dream about becoming a professional player and playing with São Paulo and maybe one match for the Brazilian national team. But the Bible says that life gives you more than you ask for, and that is what has happened to me."

Kaká was on top of the soccer world at the end of 2007. As far as his career went, there were only two questions: Could he remain there? And if so, for how long?

A New Challenge

Kaká's soccer success in 2007 was so grand that it had a big impact on him the following year—and even beyond. In February 2008, Milan decided to sign their star midfielder to a new contract that would keep him with the Rossoneri—the team's nickname that means "the red and blacks"—until 2013. Kaká told the *Milan Channel*, "Today I can say it. I want to stay with the Rossoneri for all of my career. I want to stay for life. This is my fifth season at Milan and I want to become a symbol, a standard-bearer and one day a captain of this club."

In May, Kaká was named to the *Time* 100, the American magazine's annual list of the most influential people in

Even though it looked as if Milan and Kaká wouldn't accept any transfer offers, Real Madrid made both parties an offer that neither one could pass up.

the world. Others on *Time*'s list in 2008 included future president Barack Obama, Oprah Winfrey, Facebook founder Mark Zuckerberg, and the Dalai Lama. Each of *Time*'s honorees received an article about them in a special issue of the magazine. Kaká's article was written by legendary American soccer goalie Kasey Keller. "He is the total footballer," Keller wrote. "… in an age in which many professional athletes care more about cars, women, and controversy, it's refreshing to see one who is committed to having a positive impact on the world around him."

Kaká and Caroline's first son was born June 10, 2008, at a hospital in São Paulo. They named him Luca Celico Leite. Pictures of mother and father snuggling were released to the media, along with a statement: "Mother and child are fine."

Kaká was back on the soccer field, wearing Milan's red and black, two months after Luca's birth. He picked up where he left off, scoring fifteen goals in thirty league matches, and finishing eighth in the Ballon d'Or voting. Kaká's team, however, did not fare as well as it had the previous year. Milan only finished fifth in league play.

Despite struggling with a few nagging injuries, Kaká scored a career-high sixteen league goals during the next season, 2008–09. Milan, however, still could not win the league title. Kaká—and the team—had to deal with at least one major distraction that season that possibly affected the way they performed. The rumors that other teams

When Real Madrid signed Kaká and Cristiano Ronaldo, there were many people who believed Real Madrid would now be unbeatable.

wanted to buy Kaká from Milan had not let up much in the past few years. It seemed as if teams always were inquiring about his services. Even the long-term contract he signed in early 2008 had done little to quiet them. Of all the offers and alleged offers for Kaká, the one that came in January 2009 from Manchester City was the loudest.

The English Premier League team set the soccer world abuzz when it offered Milan $150 million for the rights to Kaká. The offer was more than twice as much as any other team had ever paid to transfer a player. Milan fans were outraged at the thought of losing Kaká. Many gathered in public to protest the possible move. Some one thousand of them rallied outside Milan's team headquarters. Others stood and chanted outside his home. Although it appeared at one point like the deal would be made and Kaká would be playing in Manchester, it eventually fell through. Afterward, Kaká told *The Guardian*, "... many people showed me their support, I have received drawings by kids trying to convince me to stay. It was wonderful. I remember when I left São Paolo some fans protested against me, here they all stand by my side instead." Kaká later said those fans—and the fact that he was in the middle of a season— are what kept him from approving of the Manchester deal.

When other teams saw how close Manchester had come to getting Kaká, they began making their own offers. Milan, which was having money problems, considered them all. In June 2009, Spanish club Real Madrid's offer was accepted. Madrid paid Milan roughly $90 million for Kaká. Although the deal was for less money than Manchester had offered, it still set a world record. Kaká said he chose to go to Real Madrid because he felt the team appeared to be on the rise. He was not the only one who felt that way. Shortly after Kaká was signed, Real Madrid acquired superstar Cristiano Ronaldo, for an even higher transfer fee, to be his teammate. Both players came to Madrid in hopes of winning several titles together there. It looked like all the pieces were in place to do so.

Kaká left Milan under good terms. He told *The Guardian*: "Everything I've always done for Milan has been by mutual agreement, from the moment I arrived until my departure today. I'm leaving by the front door. I've won everything that I wanted as a player and this is a new motivation for me."

Milan issued its own statement about what it meant for a player like Kaká to leave: "His loss on the field, though serious, can be filled. It will, however, be very difficult to fill the void left by Kaká the man."

A World Cup Homecoming?

Milan's statement upon Kaká's departure was more proof that the nice-guy persona Kaká was known for was genuine. Throughout his career, when the opportunity presented itself, Kaká always had stepped up to help others in need. After he first moved from São Paulo to Milan in 2004, Kaká became the youngest "Ambassador Against Hunger" for the United Nations' World Food Program. As an ambassador, Kaká used his celebrity to gather compassion and money to feed and motivate hungry children across the world. Kaká told *The New York Times* he hoped to "… inspire hungry children to believe they can overcome the odds and lead a normal life." Over

All Villareal's goaltender can do is watch the ball roll back out from the goal as Kaká celebrates his score.

the years, Kaká has been involved with several other good causes, as well, including the Special Olympics. Much of Kaká's charity work has centered on helping poor children.

On the field with Real Madrid, Kaká handled the pressure of his new role well. He scored 8 goals in 31 league games his first season there. Those totals were a big drop-off from his numbers the previous year in Milan, but there was a valid reason for that. In Real Madrid, Kaká was playing alongside prolific goal-scorer Cristiano Ronaldo. Ronaldo played the position of forward. The main—sometimes the only—objective of a forward is to score goals. Meanwhile, Kaká played the position of midfielder. Midfielders need to be versatile players who try to score goals but also spend their time looking to help forwards score those goals. Midfielders also need to be able to play defense. Ronaldo scored 33 goals that year. Another reason Kaká's scoring was down his first season in Madrid was that he played most of the year with pain in his left knee.

Kaká fought through the knee pain during Madrid's season. Then he went on to join his home country of Brazil and compete for the 2010 World Cup in South Africa. Kaká played well in the tournament. But Brazil fell short of expectations and lost to the Netherlands in the quarterfinal round, knocking them out of the tournament.

Kaká had surgery on his knee after the World Cup. The doctor who performed the surgery said that by playing in the World Cup, Kaká could have injured himself so badly that his career would have been over. The surgery was a success but left Kaká unable to play soccer for four months. It was the first time he had been away from the field that long since he was a young child. "I'm dying to play again," he told *Ricardo-Kaka.com*. "It is very difficult to watch games because I really want to jump into the field and help my teammates in a very direct way. But I know that I must be patient..."

Kaká was away from the game a total of eight months. His first game back was in January 2011, and he played the rest of Madrid's league season. It was mostly up and down. There were a few personal highlights, but Kaká also suffered small injuries that kept him out of several games. Real Madrid lost the league title to FC Barcelona but later defeated Barcelona to win the Copa del Rey, the tournament that included all Spanish teams. Three days after the Copa del Rey, on April 23, 2011, Caroline gave birth to she and Kaká's second child, Isabella.

Real Madrid did win its league title the following year, 2011–12, as Kaká played in twenty-seven matches and scored five goals. The following year, mostly because of injuries, Kaká played in just sixteen league matches and only scored two goals. But even when Kaká was not hurt, Madrid's coach often would choose to play younger players instead of him. The lack of playing time that Kaká, someone who once was such a superstar, was receiving did not go unnoticed. Reporters and fans frequently asked Kaká if he was happy in Real Madrid or if he wanted to go to another team that would allow him to play more. Several

After agreeing upon a contract to go back to AC Milan, Kaká is formally reintroduced to the city of Milan. He was given nothing short of a hero's welcome.

other teams were named as possible suitors. Returns to Milan and Brazil were mentioned. So was playing Major League Soccer in the United States. If he came to the United States, he could even possibly play alongside his brother, Digão, who was with the New York Red Bulls.

As the controversies over his professional career continued, Kaká returned to Brazil in mid-2013 to train with the national team in preparation for the 2014 World Cup. If Kaká would have made the team—which was not guaranteed—it would have been his fourth. The Cup would have held another special meaning for the Latin-American star: the tournament was hosted by his home country of Brazil.

Had Kaká made the World Cup team, the hero's welcome that would have greeted him in every city he played in would have been huge. Not making the World Cup team hasn't stopped Kaká from wanting to play professionally still.

"I have two years left on my contract," Kaká told *Reuters* in mid-2013. "I am happy to continue at Real [Madrid], but I don't want to be a problem for the club. If I have to go, I will go."

In September 2013, after a free transfer from Real Madrid, Kaká and AC Milan agreed upon a deal that would bring the star back to Milan on a two-year contract.

Whenever Kaká ends his career, one thing is certain: He will end it as one of the best to ever have played the game of soccer.

Career Highlights and Awards

- FIFA World Cup champion: 2002
- Serie A champion (with AC Milan): 2003–04
- Supercoppa Italiana champion (with AC Milan): 2004
- Serie A Footballer of the Year: 2004, 2007
- UEFA Champions League Best Midfielder: 2004–05
- FIFA Confederations Cup champion: 2005, 2009
- FIFPro World XI: 2006, 2007, 2008
- UEFA Champions League champion (with AC Milan): 2006–07
- Pallone d'Argento Award: 2006–07
- UEFA Champions League Top Scorer: 2006–07
- UEFA Champions League Best Forward: 2006–07
- UEFA Club Footballer of the Year: 2006–07
- UEFA Super Cup champion (with AC Milan): 2007
- FIFA Club World Cup champion (with AC Milan): 2007
- FIFA Club World Cup Golden Ball: 2007
- FIFA World Player of the Year: 2007
- FIFPro World Player of the Year: 2007
- Ballon d'Or: 2007

- Onze d'Or: 2007
- FIFA Confederations Cup Golden Ball: 2009
- Marca Leyenda Award: 2009
- Copa del Rey champion (with Real Madrid): 2010–11
- La Liga champion (with Real Madrid): 2011–12
- Supercopa de España champion (with Real Madrid): 2012

INTERNET ADDRESSES

Kaká's Official Web site
<http://www.kakaww.com/>

AC Milan Official Web site
<http://www.acmilan.com/en>

FIFA Official Site
<http://www.fifa.com/>

INDEX